C

Pictures from Brueghel

and other poems

By William Carlos Williams (in print)

The Autobiography
The Build-up
Collected Earlier Poems
Collected Later Poems
The Farmers' Daughters
I Wanted to Write a Poem*
In the American Grain
In the Money
Kora in Hell: Improvisations†
Many Loves and Other Plays
Paterson, Books 1-5
Pictures from Brueghel and Other Poems
The Selected Essays
The Selected Letters§
Selected Poems
White Mule
Yes, Mrs. Williams§

* *Beacon Press*
† *City Lights Books*
§ *Ivan Obolensky*

Pictures from Brueghel

and other poems by

WILLIAM
CARLOS
WILLIAMS

Collected Poems 1950-1962

A NEW DIRECTIONS BOOK

Of the poems in this volume, the "Pictures from Brueghel" sequence
first appeared in *The Hudson Review*. Others appeared originally in the
following magazines, to which acknowledgment is here made:
*The Atlantic Monthly, Art News Annual, Botteghe Oscure, Chicago
Review, College Music Symposium* of the Moravian Music Foundation,
Inc., *East & West, Epoch, Folio, Harper's, Hudson Review, Imagi,
Kavita, The Kenyon Review, London Times Literary Supplement,
Massachusetts Review, National Review, New England Galaxy, New
Poems by American Poets, New Ventures, New World Writing, New
York Times Book Review, The New Yorker, Origin, Pennsylvania
Literary Review, Poetry, Poetry Australia, Quarterly Review of
Literature, Saturday Review, 7 Arts, Transatlantic Review.*

Acknowledgment is also made to The Lockwood Memorial Library,
University of Buffalo, and The Yale University Library for access
to their collections of Williams manuscripts.

Library of Congress Catalog Card Number: 62-10410.
First published as ND Paperbook 118 in 1962.
Clothbound edition, 1967.

Manufactured in the United States of America.
New Directions Books are published for James Laughlin
by New Directions Publishing Corporation,
333 Sixth Avenue, New York 10014.

FOURTH PRINTING

Contents

Pictures from Brueghel

". . . the form of a man's rattle may be in
accordance with instructions received in the
dream by which he obtained his power."

Frances Densmore
The Study of Indian Music

Pictures from Brueghel

I SELF-PORTRAIT

In a red winter hat blue
eyes smiling
just the head and shoulders

crowded on the canvas
arms folded one
big ear the right showing

the face slightly tilted
a heavy wool coat
with broad buttons

gathered at the neck reveals
a bulbous nose
but the eyes red-rimmed

from over-use he must have
driven them hard
but the delicate wrists

show him to have been a
man unused to
manual labor unshaved his

blond beard half trimmed
no time for any-
thing but his painting

Bruisel

According to Brueghel
when Icarus fell
it was spring.

a farmer was ploughing
his field,
the whole pageantry

of the year was
awake, tingling
near

the edge of the sea
concerned
with itself

sweating in the sun
that melted
the wings' wax

unsignificantly
off the coast
there was

a splash quite unnoticed
this was
Icarus drowning

III   THE HUNTERS IN THE SNOW

The over-all picture is winter
icy mountains
in the background the return

from the hunt it is toward evening
from the left
sturdy hunters lead in

their pack the inn-sign
hanging from a
broken hinge is a stag a crucifix

between his antlers the cold
inn yard is
deserted but for a huge bonfire

that flares wind-driven tended by
women who cluster
about it to the right beyond

the hill is a pattern of skaters
Brueghel the painter
concerned with it all has chosen

a winter-struck bush for his
foreground to
complete the picture .   .

From the Nativity
which I have already celebrated
the Babe in its Mother's arms

the Wise Men in their stolen
splendor
and Joseph and the soldiery

attendant
with their incredulous faces
make a scene copied we'll say

from the Italian masters
but with a difference
the mastery

of the painting
and the mind the resourceful mind
that governed the whole

the alert mind dissatisfied with
what it is asked to
and cannot do

accepted the story and painted
it in the brilliant
colors of the chronicler

the downcast eyes of the Virgin
as a work of art
for profound worship

V PEASANT WEDDING

Pour the wine bridegroom
where before you the
bride is enthroned her hair

loose at her temples a head
of ripe wheat is on
the wall beside her the

guests seated at long tables
the bagpipers are ready
there is a hound under

the table the bearded Mayor
is present women in their
starched headgear are

gabbing all but the bride
hands folded in her
lap is awkwardly silent simple

dishes are being served
clabber and what not
from a trestle made of an

unhinged barn door by two
helpers one in a red
coat a spoon in his hatband

VI HAYMAKING

The living quality of
the man's mind
stands out

and its covert assertions
for art, art, art!
painting

that the Renaissance
tried to absorb
but

it remained a wheat field
over which the
wind played

men with scythes tumbling
the wheat in
rows

the gleaners already busy
it was his own—
magpies

the patient horses no one
could take that
from him

Summer!
the painting is organized
about a young

reaper enjoying his
noonday rest
completely

relaxed
from his morning labors
sprawled

in fact sleeping
unbuttoned
on his back

the women
have brought him his lunch
perhaps

a spot of wine
they gather gossiping
under a tree

whose shade
carelessly
he does not share the

resting
center of
their workaday world

Disciplined by the artist
to go round
& round

in holiday gear
a riotously gay rabble of
peasants and their

ample-bottomed doxies
fills
the market square

featured by the women in
their starched
white headgear

they prance or go openly
toward the wood's
edges

round and around in
rough shoes and
farm breeches

mouths agape
Oya!
kicking up their heels

This horrible but superb painting
the parable of the blind
without a red

in the composition shows a group
of beggars leading
each other diagonally downward

across the canvas
from one side
to stumble finally into a bog

where the picture
and the composition ends back
of which no seeing man

is represented the unshaven
features of the des-
titute with their few

pitiful possessions a basin
to wash in a peasant
cottage is seen and a church spire

the faces are raised
as toward the light
there is no detail extraneous

to the composition one
follows the others stick in
hand triumphant to disaster

I

This is a schoolyard
crowded
with children

of all ages near a village
on a small stream
meandering by

where some boys
are swimming
bare-ass

or climbing a tree in leaf
everything
is motion

elder women are looking
after the small
fry

a play wedding a
christening
nearby one leans

hollering
into
an empty hogshead

Little girls
whirling their skirts about
until they stand out flat

tops pinwheels
to run in the wind with
or a toy in 3 tiers to spin

with a piece
of twine to make it go
blindman's-buff follow the

leader stilts
high and low tipcat jacks
bowls hanging by the knees

standing on your head
run the gauntlet
a dozen on their backs

feet together kicking
through which a boy must pass
roll the hoop or a

construction
made of bricks
some mason has abandoned

The desperate toys
of children
their

imagination equilibrium
and rocks
which are to be

found
everywhere
and games to drag

the other down
blindfold
to make use of

a swinging
weight
with which

at random
to bash in the
heads about

them
Brueghel saw it all
and with his grim

humor faithfully
recorded
it

Exercise

Maybe it's his wife
the car is an official car
belonging

to a petty police officer
I think
but her get-up

was far from official
for that time
of day

Song

beauty is a shell
from the sea
where she rules triumphant
till love has had its way with her

scallops and
lion's paws
sculptured to the
tune of retreating waves

undying accents
repeated till
the ear and the eye lie
down together in the same bed

The Woodthrush

fortunate man it is not too late
the woodthrush
flies into my garden

before the snow
he looks at me silent without
moving

his dappled breast reflecting
tragic winter
thoughts my love my own

The Polar Bear

his coat resembles the snow
deep snow
the male snow
which attacks and kills

silently as it falls muffling
the world
to sleep that
the interrupted quiet return

to lie down with us
its arms
about our necks
murderously a little while

The Loving Dexterity

The flower
fallen
she saw it

where
it lay
a pink petal

intact
deftly
placed it

on
its stem
again

The Chrysanthemum

how shall we tell
the bright petals
from the sun in the
sky concentrically

crowding the branch
save that it yields
· in its modesty
to that splendor?

3 Stances

I: ELAINE

poised for the leap she
is not yet ready for
—save in her eyes

her bare toes
starting over the clipt
lawn where she may

not go emphasize summer
and the curl
of her blonde hair

the tentative smile
for the adult plans laid
to trap her

calves beginning to flex
wrists
set for the getaway

II: ERICA

the melody line is
everything
in this composition

when I first witnessed
your head
and held it

admiringly between
my fingers
I bowed

my approval
at the Scandinavian
name they'd

given you Erica after
your father's
forebears

the rest remains a
mystery
your snub nose spinning

on the bridge of it
points the way
inward

III: EMILY

your long legs
built
to carry high

the small head
your
grandfather

knows
if he knows
anything

gives
the dance as
your genius

the cleft in
your
chin's curl

permitting
may it
carry you far

Suzy

I

women your age have decided
wars and the beat
of poems your grandfather

is a poet and loves you
pay attention
to your lessons an inkling

of what beauty means to
a girl your age
may dawn soon upon you

II

life is a flower when it
opens you will
look trembling into it unsure

of what the traditional
mirror may reveal
between hope and despair while

a timorous old man
doubtfully half
turns away his foolish head

III

a bunch of violets clutched
in your idle
hand gives him a place

beside you which he cherishes
his back turned
from you casually appearing

not to look he yearns after
you protectively
hopelessly wanting nothing

I

when you shall arrive
as deep
as you will need go

to catch the blackfish
the hook
has been featly baited

by the art you have
and
you do catch them

II

with what thoroughness
you know
seize that glistening

body translated
to
that language you

will understand gut
clean
roast garnish and

III

serve to yourself who
better
eat and enjoy

however you
divide
and share

that blackfish heft
and shine
is your own

Fragment

as for him who
finds fault
may silliness

and sorrow
overtake him
when you wrote

you did not
know
the power of

your words

To a Woodpecker

December bird in the bare tree
your harsh cry sounds
reminding me

of death we celebrated by lamen-
tations crying out
in the old

days wails of anguish shrieking
wakes curses that the
gods

had been so niggardly sweet
nightingale of the
winter

woods hang out the snow as if
it were gay
curtains

Song

I'd rather read an account
of a hidden
Carolina swamp where

the white heron breeds
protected from
the hunters reached only across

half-sunken logs a place
difficult of access the females
building their nests

in the stifling heat the males
in their mating splendor
than to witness

her broad pelvis
making her awkward at the
getaway . . .

but I have forgot beauty
that is no more than a sop
when our time

is spent and infirmities
bring us to
eat out of the same bowl!

The Children

Once in a while
we'd find a patch
of yellow violets

not many
but blue big blue
ones in

the cemetery woods
we'd pick
bunches of them

there was a family
named Foltette
a big family

with lots of children's graves
so we'd take

bunches of violets
and place one
on each headstone

The Painting

Starting from black or
finishing
with it

her defeat stands
a delicate
lock

of blonde hair dictated
by the
Sorbonne

this was her last
clear
act

a portrait of a
child
to which

she was indifferent
beautifully
drawn

then she married and
moved to
another country

The Stone Crock

In my hand I hold
a postcard
addressed to me
     by a lady

Stoneware crock
salt-glazed
a dandelion embossed
     dark blue

She selected it
for me to
admire casually
     in passing

she was a Jewess
intimate of
a man I
     admired

We often met in
her studio
and talked
     of him

he loved the early
art of this
country
     blue stoneware

stamped on the
bulge of it
Albany reminding me
     of him

Now he is dead how
gentle he
was and
      persistent

He Has Beaten about the Bush Long Enough

What a team
Flossie, Mary, a chemistry prof
and I

make to confront
the
slowly hardening

brain
of an academician
The most

that can be said
for it
is

that it has the crystal-
line pattern
of

new ice on
a country
pool

Iris

a burst of iris so that
come down for
breakfast

we searched through the
rooms for
that

sweetest odor and at
first could not
find its

source then a blue as
of the sea
struck

startling us from among
those trumpeting
petals

Song

you are forever April
to me
the eternally unready

forsythia a blonde
straight-
legged girl

whom I myself
ignorant
as I was taught

to read the poems
my arms
about your neck

we clung together
peril-
ously

more than a young
girl
should know

a burst of frost
nipped
yellow flowers

in the spring
of
the year

The Dance

When the snow falls the flakes
spin upon the long axis
that concerns them most intimately
two and two to make a dance

the mind dances with itself,
taking you by the hand,
your lover follows
there are always two,

yourself and the other,
the point of your shoe setting the pace,
if you break away and run
the dance is over

Breathlessly you will take
another partner
better or worse who will keep
at your side, at your stops

whirls and glides until he too
leaves off
on his way down as if
there were another direction

gayer, more carefree
spinning face to face but always down
with each other secure
only in each other's arms

But only the dance is sure!
make it your own.
Who can tell
what is to come of it?

in the woods of your
own nature whatever
twig interposes, and bare twigs
have an actuality of their own

this flurry of the storm
that holds us,
plays with us and discards us
dancing, dancing as may be credible.

Jersey Lyric

view of winter trees
before
one tree

in the foreground
where
by fresh-fallen

snow
lie 6 woodchunks ready
for the fire

To the Ghost of Marjorie Kinnan Rawlings

To celebrate your brief life
as you lived it grimly
under attack as it happens
to any common soldier
black or white
surrounded by the heavy scent
of orange blossoms solitary
in your low-lying farm among the young trees

Wise and gentle-voiced
old colored women
attended you among the reeds
and polonia
with its blobs of purple
flowers your pup smelling of
skunk beside your grove-men
lovesick maids and
one friend of the same sex
who knew how to handle a boat in a swamp

Your quick trips to your
New York publisher
beating your brains out
over the composition
under the trees to the tune
of a bull got loose
gathering the fruit and
preparing new fields to be put under the plough

You lived nerves drawn
tense beside dogtooth violets
bougainvillaea swaying
rushes and yellow jasmine

that smells so sweet
young and desperate
as you were taking chances
sometimes that you should be
thrown from the saddle
and get your neck broke
as it must have happened and it did in the end

To Be Recited to Flossie on Her Birthday

Let him who may
among the continuing lines
seek out

that tortured constancy
affirms
where I persist

let me say
across cross purposes
that the flower bloomed

struggling to assert itself
simply under
the conflicting lights

you will believe me
a rose
to the end of time

Metric Figure

gotta hold your nose
with the appropriate gesture
smiling

back of
the garbage truck
as the complex

city passes
to the confession
or psychiatric couch or booth

The Intelligent Sheepman and the New Cars

I'd like to
pull
the back out

and use
one of them
to take

my "girls"
to
the fairs in

The Italian Garden

When she married years ago
her romantic ideas dominated
the builders

nightingale and hermit thrush
then the garden
fell into disuse.

Now her son has taken up her
old ideas formally
shut out

by high walls from the sheep run.
It is a scene from Comus
transported

to upper New York State. I remember
it already ruined
in

early May the trees crowded
with orioles chickadees
robins

brown-thrashers cardinals
in their scarlet
coats

vocal at dawn among pools
reft of their
lilies

and rarer plants flowers
given instead to
mallows

pampas-grass and cattails by
drought and winter
winds

where now hummingbirds touch
without touching.
Moss-covered

benches fallen apart among
sunken gardens
where

The Faerie Queene was read to
strains from
Campion

and the scent of wild strawberries
mingled with that
of eglantine

and verbena. Courtesy has revived
with visitors who
have

begun to stroll the paths
as in the quattrocentro
covertly.

Maybe it will drive them to
be more civil
love

more jocosely (a good word) as
we presume they did
in that famous

garden where Boccaccio and
his friends hid
themselves

from the plague and rude manners
in the woods
of that garden

as we would similarly today
to escape the plague
of

our cars which cannot
penetrate
hers.

Poem

The rose fades
and is renewed again
by its seed, naturally
but where

save in the poem
shall it go
to suffer no diminution
of its splendor

A Formal Design

This fleur-de-lis
at a fence rail
where a unicorn is

confined it is a tapestry
deftly woven
a milleflor

design the fleur-de-lis
with its yellow
petals edges

a fruiting tree formally
enough in
this climate

a pomegranate to which
a princely
collar round his

arching neck the beast
is lightly
tethered

Bird

Bird with outstretched
wings poised
inviolate unreaching

yet reaching
your image this November
planes

to a stop
miraculously fixed in my
arresting eyes

The Gossips

Blocking the sidewalk so
we had to go round
3 carefully coiffured
and perfumed old men
fresh from the barbers
a cartoon by Daumier
reflecting the times were
discussing with a foreign
accent one cupping his
ears not to miss a
syllable the news from
Russia on a view of
the reverse surface of
the moon   .

Exercise No. 2

The metal smokestack
of my neighbor's chimney
greets me among the new leaves

it is a small house
adjacent to my bigger one
I have come in 3 years

to know much of her
an old lady as I am an old man
we greet each other

across the hedge
my wife gives her flowers
we have never visited each other

The World Contracted to a Recognizable Image

at the small end of an illness
there was a picture
probably Japanese
which filled my eye

an idiotic picture
except it was all I recognized
the wall lived for me in that picture
I clung to it as to a fly

The Fruit

Waking
I was eating pears!
she said

I sat beside her on the bed
thinking
of Picasso

a portrait of
a sensitive young boy
gathered

into himself
Waking
I was eating pears!

she said
when separate jointly
we embraced

Short Poem

You slapped my face
oh but so gently
I smiled
at the caress

43

Poem

on getting a card
long delayed
from a poet whom I love
but

with whom I differ
touching
the modern poetic
technique

I was much moved
to hear
from him if
as yet he does not

concede the point
nor is he
indeed conscious of it
no matter

his style
has other outstanding
virtues
which delight me

To Flossie

who showed me
                a bunch of garden roses
she was keeping
                on ice

against an appointment
                with friends
for supper
                day after tomorrow

aren't they beautiful
                you can't
smell them
                because they're so cold

but aren't they
                in wax
paper for the
                moment beautiful

Portrait of a Woman at Her Bath

it is a satisfaction
a joy
to have one of those
in the house

when she takes a bath
she unclothes
herself she is no
Venus

I laugh at her
an Inca
shivering at the well
the sun is

glad of a fellow to
marvel at
the birds and the flowers
look in

Some Simple Measures in the American Idiom and the Variable Foot

I: EXERCISE IN TIMING

Oh
the sumac died
it's
the first time
I
noticed it

II: HISTOLOGY

There is
the
microscopic
anatomy

of
the whale
this is
reassuring

III: PERPETUUM MOBILE

To all the girls
of all ages
who walk up and down on

the streets of this town
silent or gabbing
putting

their feet down
one before the other
one two

one two they
pause sometimes before
a store window and

reform the line
from here
to China everywhere

back and
forth and back and forth
and back and forth

IV: THE BLUE JAY

It crouched
just before the take-off

caught
in the cinematograph—

in motion
of the mind wings

just set to spread a
flash a

blue curse
a memory of you

my friend
shrieked at me

—serving art
as usual

V: THE EXISTENTIALIST'S WIFE

I used to follow
the seasons
in this semi-northern

climate
and the warblers
that come

in May knew
the parula from
the myrtle

when I found it
dead on
the lawn there is

no season but
the one
for me now

VI: A SALAD FOR THE SOUL

My pleasant soul
we may not be destined to
survive our guts
let's celebrate

what we eject
sometimes

49

with greatest fervor
I hear it

also from the ladies' room
what ho!
the source
of all delicious salads

VII: CHLOE

The calves of
the young girls legs
when they are well made

knees
lithely built
in their summer clothes

show them
predisposed toward flight
or the dance

the magenta flower
of the
moth-mullen balanced

idly
tilting her weight
from one foot

to the other
shifting
to avoid looking at me

on my way to
mail a letter
smiling to a friend

VIII: THE COCKTAIL PARTY

A young woman
on whose belly I have never
slept though others

have
met today
at a cocktail party

not drunk
but by love
ignoring the others

we looked in
each other's eyes
eyes alert to

what we were saying
eyes blinded
breathless by that alone

IX: THE STOLEN PEONIES

What I got out of women
was difficult
to assess Flossie

not you
you lived with me
many years you remember

that year
we had the magnificent
stand of peonies

how happy we were
with them
but one night

they were stolen
we shared the
loss together thinking

of nothing else for
a whole day
nothing could have

brought us closer
we had been
married ten years

The High Bridge above the
Tagus River at Toledo

A young man, alone, on the high bridge over the Tagus which
    was too narrow to allow the sheep driven by the lean,
    enormous dogs whose hind legs worked slowly on cogs
to pass easily . . .
        (he didn't speak the language)

Pressed against the parapet either side by the crowding sheep,
    the relentless pressure of the dogs communicated
    itself to him also
above the waters in the gorge below.

They were hounds to him rather than sheep dogs because of
    their size and savage appearance, dog tired from the day's
    work.
The stiff jerking movement of the hind legs, the hanging
    heads at the shepherd's heels, slowly followed the excited
    and crowding sheep.

The whole flock, the shepherd and the dogs, were covered
    with dust as if they had been all day long on the road. The
    pace of the sheep, slow in the mass,
governed the man and the dogs. They were approaching the
    city at nightfall, the long journey completed.

In old age they walk in the old man's dreams and still walk
    in his dreams, peacefully continuing in his verse
    forever.

15 Years Later

on seeing my own play
Many Loves
on the stage for the first time

I recall
many a passage
of the original con-

versations with my
patients, especially the
women, myself

the interlocutor
laying myself bare for them
all there

in the play but who will
take the trouble
to evaluate

the serious aspects of
the case? One
of the actors by

dint of learning the lines
by heart
has come to me

his face aglow openmouthed
a light in his eyes
Nothing more

The Title

—as in Gauguin's *The Loss of Virginity*—
how inessential it is to the composition:

the nude body, unattended save by a watchful
hound, forepaw against the naked breast,

there she lies on her back in an open field,
limbs quietly assembled—yet how by its

very unrelatedness it enhances the impact
and emotional dignity of the whole . . .

Mounted as an Amazon

She rides her hips as
it were a horse
such women

tickle me a pat answer
to philosophy
or high heels would

put them on their
cans if fol-
lowed up most women

are more pliant
come of
a far different race

The Snow Begins

A rain of bombs, well placed,
is no less lovely
but this comes gently over all

all crevices are covered
the stalks of
fallen flowers vanish before

this benefice all the garden's
wounds are healed
white, white, white as death

fallen which dignifies it as
no violence ever can
gently and silently in the night.

Calypsos

I

Well God is
love
so love me

God
is love so
love me God

is
love so love
me well

II

Love the sun
comes
up in

the morning
and
in

the evening
zippy zappy
it goes

III

We watched
a red rooster
with

two hens
back
of the museum

at
St. Croix
flap his

wings
zippy zappy
and crow

An Exercise

Sick as I am
confused in the head
I mean I have

endured this April
so far
visiting friends

returning home
late at night
I saw

a huge Negro
a dirty collar
about his

enormous neck
appeared to be
choking

him
I did not know
whether or not

he saw me though
he was sitting
directly

before me how
shall we
escape this modern

age
and learn
to breathe again

Three Nahuatl Poems

One by one I proclaim your songs:
    I bind them on, gold crabs, as if they were anklets:
    like emeralds I gather them.
Clothe yourself in them: they are your riches.
    Bathe in feathers of the quetzal,
your treasury of birds' plumes, black and yellow,
the red feathers of the macaw
beat your drums about the world:
deck yourself out in them: they are your riches.

Where am I to go, whither?
    The road's there, the road to Two-Gods.
    Well, who checks men here,
here where all lack a body,
at the bottom of the sky?
Or, maybe, it is only on Earth
that we lose the body?
    Cleaned out, rid of it completely,
His House: there remains none on this earth!
Who is it that said:
Where find them? our friends no longer exist!

Will he return will Prince Cuautli ever return?
Will Ayocuan, the one who drove an arrow into the sky?
Shall these two yet gladden you?
    Events don't recur: we vanish once only.
Hence the cause of my weeping:
Prince Ayocuan, warrior chief
governed us harshly.
His pride waxed more, he grew haughty
here among men.
    But his time is finished . . .

he can no longer come to bow down before Father and
    Mother. . . .
This is the reason for my weeping:
He has fled to the place where all lack a body.

Sonnet in Search of an Author

Nude bodies like peeled logs
sometimes give off a sweetest
odor, man and woman

under the trees in full excess
matching the cushion of

aromatic pine-drift fallen
threaded with trailing woodbine
a sonnet might be made of it

Might be made of it! odor of excess
odor of pine needles, odor of
peeled logs, odor of no odor
other than trailing woodbine that

has no odor, odor of a nude woman
sometimes, odor of a man.

The Gift

As the wise men of old brought gifts
        guided by a star
               to the humble birthplace

of the god of love,
        the devils
             as an old print shows
retreated in confusion.

        What could a baby know
             of gold ornaments
or frankincense and myrrh,
        of priestly robes
             and devout genuflections?

But the imagination
        knows all stories
             before they are told
and knows the truth of this one
        past all defection

The rich gifts
        so unsuitable for a child
             though devoutly proffered,
stood for all that love can bring.

        The men were old
             how could they know
of a mother's needs
        or a child's
        appetite?

But as they kneeled
        the child was fed.

They saw it
and
gave praise!

A miracle
had taken place,
hard gold to love,
a mother's milk!
before
their wondering eyes.

The ass brayed
the cattle lowed.
It was their nature.

All men by their nature give praise.
It is all
they can do.

The very devils
by their flight give praise.
What is death,
beside this?

Nothing. The wise men
came with gifts
and bowed down
to worship
this perfection.

The Turtle

(For My Grandson)

Not because of his eyes,
        the eyes of a bird,
                but because he is beaked,
birdlike, to do an injury,
        has the turtle attracted you.
                He is your only pet.
When we are together
        you talk of nothing else
                ascribing all sorts
of murderous motives
        to his least action.
                You ask me
to write a poem,
        should I have poems to write,
                about a turtle.

The turtle lives in the mud
        but is not mud-like,
                you can tell it by his eyes
which are clear.
        When he shall escape
                his present confinement
he will stride about the world
        destroying all
                with his sharp beak.
Whatever opposes him
        in the streets of the city
                shall go down.
Cars will be overturned.
        And upon his back
                shall ride,

to his conquests,
          my Lord,
                you!

You shall be master!
        In the beginning
                there was a great tortoise
who supported the world.
        Upon him
                all ultimately
rests.
        Without him
                nothing will stand.
He is all wise
        and can outrun the hare.
                In the night
his eyes carry him
        to unknown places.
                He is your friend.

Sappho, Be Comforted

There is only one love
let it be a sparrow
to hold between the breasts
     greets us daily with its small cries

what does it matter?
I, we'll say, love a woman
but truth to tell
     I love myself more. Sappho loves

the music of her own
songs which men seldom
mean to her, a lovely girl
     of whom she is desperately fond:

This is myself though
my hateful mirror
shows every day my big nose.
     Men are indifferent to me, my sweet

but I would not trade
my skill in composition for
all, a second choice, you
     present for my passionate caresses.

or he were a Jew or a
Welshman
I hope they do give you the Nobel Prize
it would serve you right
            —in perpetuity
with such a name

If I were a dog
I'd sit down on a cold pavement
in the rain
to wait for a friend (and so would you)
if it so pleased me
even if it were January or Zukofsky

Your English
is not specific enough
As a writer of poems
you show yourself to be inept not to say
usurious

Tapiola

He is no more dead than Finland herself is dead
under the blows of the mass-man who threatened
to destroy her until she felled her forests
about his head, ensnaring him. But, children, you
underestimated the power in your own song, *Finlandia!*
It holds you up but no more so than has he I celebrate
who had heard the icy wind in his ears and defied
it lovingly with a smile. The power of music,
of composition, the placing of sounds together,
edge against edge, Musorgski the half-mad Russian
had it and Dostoevski who knew the soul. In such
style whistled the winds grateful to be tamed,
we say, by a man. Whee-wow! You stayed up half
the night in your attic room under the eaves, composing
secretly, setting it down, period after period,
as the wind whistled. Lightning flashed! The roof
creaked about your ears threatening to give
way! But you had a composition to finish that could
not wait. The storm entered your mind where all
good things are secured, written down, for love's
sake and to defy the devil of emptiness. The
children are decked out in ribbons, bunting and
with flags in their hands to celebrate your birthday!
They parade to music! a joyous occasion. Sibelius
has been born and continues to live in all our
minds, all of us, forever. . . .

Poem

The plastic surgeon who has
concerned himself
with the repair of the mole

on my ear could not be
more pointedly
employed

let all men confess it
Gauguin or Van Gogh
were intimates

who fell out finally
and parted going
to the ends of the earth

to be apart, wild men
one of them cut
his ear off with a pair of shears

which made him none the less
a surpassing genius
this happened

yesterday forgive him
he was mad
and who among us has retained

his sanity or balance
in the course the
events have taken since those days

Heel & Toe to the End

Gagarin says, in ecstasy,
he could have
gone on forever

he floated
ate and sang
and when he emerged from that

one hundred eight minutes off
the surface of
the earth he was smiling

Then he returned
to take his place
among the rest of us

from all that division and
subtraction a measure
toe and heel

heel and toe he felt
as if he had
been dancing

The Rewaking

Sooner or later
we must come to the end
of striving

to re-establish
the image the image of
the rose

but not yet
you say extending the
time indefinitely

by
your love until a whole
spring

rekindle
the violet to the very
lady's-slipper

and so by
your love the very sun
itself is revived

The Desert Music and Other Poems

(1954)

To Bill and Paul

The Descent

The descent beckons
   as the ascent beckoned.
      Memory is a kind
of accomplishment,
   a sort of renewal
     even
an initiation, since the spaces it opens are new places
   inhabited by hordes
      heretofore unrealized,
of new kinds—
   since their movements
      are toward new objectives
(even though formerly they were abandoned).

No defeat is made up entirely of defeat—since
the world it opens is always a place
   formerly
      unsuspected. A
world lost,
   a world unsuspected,
      beckons to new places
and no whiteness (lost) is so white as the memory
of whiteness .

With evening, love wakens
   though its shadows
      which are alive by reason
of the sun shining—
   grow sleepy now and drop away
     from desire .

Love without shadows stirs now
       beginning to awaken
              as night
advances.

The descent
       made up of despairs
           and without accomplishment
realizes a new awakening:
          which is a reversal
of despair.
        For what we cannot accomplish, what
is denied to love,
       what we have lost in the anticipation—
          a descent follows,
endless and indestructible   .

To Daphne and Virginia

The smell of the heat is boxwood
                when rousing us
                        a movement of the air
stirs our thoughts
                that had no life in them
                        to a life, a life in which
two women agonize:
                to live and to breathe is no less.
                        Two young women.
The box odor
                is the odor of that of which
                        partaking separately,
each to herself
                I partake also
                        .   .   separately.

Be patient that I address you in a poem,
                there is no other
                        fit medium.
The mind
                lives there. It is uncertain,
                        can trick us and leave us
agonized. But for resources
                what can equal it?
                        There is nothing. We
should be lost
                without its wings to
                        fly off upon.

The mind is the cause of our distresses
                but of it we can build anew.
                        Oh something more than

it flies off to:
          a woman's world,
                    of crossed sticks, stopping
thought. A new world
          is only a new mind.
                    And the mind and the poem
are all apiece.
          Two young women
                    to be snared,
odor of box,
          to bind and hold them
                    for the mind's labors.

All women are fated similarly
          facing men
                    and there is always
another, such as I,
          who loves them,
                    loves all women, but
finds himself, touching them,
          like other men,
                    often confused.

I have two sons,
          the husbands of these women,
                    who live also
in a world of love,
          apart.
                    Shall this odor of box in
                    the heat
not also touch them
          fronting a world of women
                    from which they are
debarred
          by the very scents which draw them on
                    against easy access?

In our family we stammer unless,
        half mad,
                we come to speech at last

And I am not
        a young man.
                My love encumbers me.
It is a love
        less than
                a young man's love but,
like this box odor
        more penetrant, infinitely
                more penetrant,
in that sense not to be resisted.

There is, in the hard
        give and take
                of a man's life with
                a woman
a thing which is not the stress itself
        but beyond
                and above
that,
        something that wants to rise
        and shake itself
free. We are not chickadees
        on a bare limb
                with a worm in the mouth.
The worm is in our brains
        and concerns them
                and not food for our
offspring, wants to disrupt
        our thought
                and throw it
to the newspapers
        or anywhere.

There is, in short,
a counter stress,
                    born of the sexual shock,
                         which survives it
consonant with the moon,
                    to keep its own mind.
                    There is, of course,
more.
               Women
                    are not alone
in that. At least
                    while this healing odor is abroad
                         one can write a poem.

Staying here in the country
                    on an old farm
                         we eat our breakfasts
on a balcony under an elm.
                    The shrubs below us
                         are neglected. And
there, penned in,
                    or he would eat the garden,
                         lives a pet goose who
tilts his head
                    sidewise
                         and looks up at us,
a very quiet old fellow
                    who writes no poems.
                         Fine mornings we sit there
while birds
                    come and go.
                         A pair of robins
is building a nest   .
                    for the second time
                         this season. Men

against their reason
        speak of love, sometimes,
                when they are old. It is
all they can do   .
        or watch a heavy goose
                who waddles, slopping
                noisily in the mud of
                his pool.

The Orchestra

The precise counterpart
            of a cacophony of bird calls
                        lifting the sun almighty
into his sphere: wood-winds
            clarinet and violins
                        sound a prolonged A!
Ah! the sun, the sun! is about to rise
            and shed his beams
                        as he has always done
upon us all,
            drudges and those
                        who live at ease,
women and men,
            upon the old,
                        upon children and the sick
who are about to die and are indeed
            dead in their beds,
                        to whom his light
is forever lost. The cello
            raises his bass note
                        manfully in the treble din:
Ah, ah and ah!
            together, unattuned
                        seeking a common tone.
Love is that common tone
            shall raise his fiery head
                        and sound his note.

The purpose of an orchestra
            is to organize those sounds
                        and hold them
to an assembled order   .
            in spite of the

                          "wrong note." Well, shall we
think or listen? Is there a sound addressed
              not wholly to the ear?
                    We half close
our eyes. We do not
           hear it through our eyes.
                  It is not
a flute note either, it is the relation
          of a flute note
                  to a drum. I am wide
awake. The mind
            is listening. The ear
                  is alerted. But the ear
in a half-reluctant mood
           stretches
                    .   .   and yawns.

And so the banked violins
           in three tiers
                  enliven the scene,
pizzicato. For a short
           memory or to
                  make the listener listen
the theme is repeated
           stressing a variant:
                  it is a principle of music
to repeat the theme. Repeat
           and repeat again,
                  as the pace mounts. The
theme is difficult   .
           but no more difficult
                  than the facts to be
resolved. Repeat
           and repeat the theme
                  and all it develops to be

until thought is dissolved
in tears.
Our dreams
have been assaulted
by a memory that will not
sleep. The
French horns
interpose
.   .   their voices:
I love you. My heart
is innocent. And this
the first day of the world!

Say to them:
"Man has survived hitherto because he was too ignorant
to know how to realize his wishes. Now that he can realize
them, he must either change them or perish."

Now is the time   .
in spite of the "wrong note"
I love you. My heart is
innocent.
And this the first
(and last) day of the world

The birds twitter now anew
but a design
surmounts their twittering.
It is a design of a man
that makes them twitter.
It is a design.

For Eleanor and Bill Monahan

Mother of God! Our Lady!
       the heart
              is an unruly Master:
Forgive us our sins
       as we
              forgive
those who have sinned against
       us.
              We submit ourselves
to Your rule
       as the flowers in May
              submit themselves to
              Your Holy rule—against
that impossible springtime
       when men
              shall be the flowers
spread at your feet.

As far as spring is
       from winter
              so are we
from you now. We have not come
       easily
              to your environs
but painfully
       across sands
              that have scored our
feet. That which we have suffered
       was for us
              to suffer. Now,
in the winter of the year,
       the birds who know how
              to escape suffering

by flight
                are gone. Man alone
                          is that creature who
cannot escape suffering
                by flight   .

I do not come to you
                save that I confess
                        to being
                        half man and half
woman. I have seen the ivy
                cling
                        to a piece of crumbled
wall so that
                you cannot tell
                        by which either
stands: this is to say
                if she to whom I cling
                        is loosened both
of us go down.

Mother of God
                I have seen you stoop
                        to a merest flower
and raise it
                and press it to your cheek.
                        I could have called out
joyfully
                but you were too far off.
                        You are a woman and
it was
                a woman's gesture.

You have no lovers now
                in the bare skies
                        to bring you flowers,

to whisper to you
                under a hedge
                                howbeit
you are young
                and fit to be loved.
                                I declare it boldly
with my heart
                in my teeth
                                and my knees knocking
together. Yet I declare
                it, and by God's word
                                it is no lie. Make us
humble and obedient to His rule.

There are men
                who as they live
                                fling caution to the
wind and women praise them
                and love them for it.
                                Cruel as the claws of
a cat   .   .

The moon which
                they have vulgarized recently
                                is still
your planet
                as it was Dian's before
                                you. What
do they think they will attain
                by their ships
                                that death has not
already given
                them? Their ships
                                should be directed
inward upon   .   But I
                am an old man. I
                                have had enough.

The female principle of the world
                    is my appeal
                              in the extremity
to which I have come.
                    O clemens! O pia! O dolcis!
                    Maria!

To a Dog Injured in the Street

It is myself,
                    not the poor beast lying there
                              yelping with pain
that brings me to myself with a start—
                    as at the explosion
                              of a bomb, a bomb that has laid
all the world waste.
                    I can do nothing
                              but sing about it
and so I am assuaged
                    from my pain.

A drowsy numbness drowns my sense
                    as if of hemlock
                              I had drunk. I think
of the poetry
                    of René Char
                              and all he must have seen
and suffered
                    that has brought him
                              to speak only of

sedgy rivers,
                of daffodils and tulips
                                whose roots they water,
even to the free-flowing river
                that laves the rootlets
                                of those sweet-scented flowers
that people the
                milky
                                way

I remember Norma
                our English setter of my childhood
                                her silky ears
and expressive eyes.
                She had a litter
                                of pups one night
in our pantry and I kicked
                one of them
                                thinking, in my alarm,
that they
                were biting her breasts
                                to destroy her.

I remember also
                a dead rabbit
                                lying harmlessly
on the outspread palm
                of a hunter's hand.
                                As I stood by
watching
                he took a hunting knife
                                and with a laugh
thrust it
                up into the animal's private parts.
                                I almost fainted.

Why should I think of that now?
            The cries of a dying dog
                        are to be blotted out
as best I can.
            René Char
                        you are a poet who believes
in the power of beauty
            to right all wrongs.
                        I believe it also.
With invention and courage
            we shall surpass
                        the pitiful dumb beasts,
let all men believe it,
            as you have taught me also
                        to believe it.

The Yellow Flower

What shall I say, because talk I must?
        That I have found a cure
               for the sick?
I have found no cure
        for the sick   .
               but this crooked flower
which only to look upon
        all men
               are cured. This
is that flower
        for which all men
               sing secretly their hymns
of praise. This
        is that sacred
               flower!

Can this be so?
        A flower so crooked
               and obscure? It is
a mustard flower
        and not a mustard flower,
               a single spray
topping the deformed stem
        of fleshy leaves
               in this freezing weather
under glass.

An ungainly flower and
        an unnatural one,
               in this climate; what
can be the reason
        that it has picked me out
               to hold me, openmouthed,

rooted before this window
                in the cold,
                                my will
drained from me
                so that I have only eyes
                                for these yellow,
twisted petals   .   ?

That the sight,
                though strange to me,
                                must be a common one,
is clear: there are such flowers
                with such leaves
                                native to some climate
which they can call
                their own.

But why the torture
                and the escape through
                                the flower? It is
as if Michelangelo
                had conceived the subject
                                of his *Slaves* from this
—or might have done so.
                And did he not make
                                the marble bloom? I
am sad
                as he was sad
                                in his heroic mood.
But also
                I have eyes
                                that are made to see and if
they see ruin for myself
                and all that I hold
                                dear, they see

also
          through the eyes
                    and through the lips
and tongue the power
          to free myself
                    and speak of it, as
Michelangelo through his hands
          had the same, if greater,
                    power.

Which leaves, to account for,
          the tortured bodies
                    of
the slaves themselves
          and
                    the tortured body of my flower
which is not a mustard flower at all
          but some unrecognized
                    and unearthly flower
for me to naturalize
          and acclimate
                    and choose it for my own.

The Host

According to their need,
        this tall Negro evangelist
                (at a table separate from the
                rest of his party);
these two young Irish nuns
        (to be described subsequently);
                and this white-haired Anglican
have come witlessly
        to partake of the host
                laid for them (and for me)
by the tired waitresses.

It is all
        (since eat we must)
                made sacred by our common need.
The evangelist's assistants
        are most open in their praise
            though covert
as would be seemly
        in such a public
            place. The nuns
are all black, a side view.
        The cleric,
            his head bowed to reveal
his unruly poll
        dines alone.

My eyes are restless.
        The evangelists eat well,
            fried oysters and what not
at this railway restaurant. The Sisters
        are soon satisfied. One
           on leaving,

looking straight before her under steadfast brows,
        reveals
                blue eyes. I myself
have brown eyes
        and a milder mouth.

There is nothing to eat,
        seek it where you will,
                but of the body of the Lord.
The blessed plants
        and the sea, yield it
                to the imagination
intact. And by that force
        it becomes real,
                bitterly
to the poor animals
        who suffer and die
                that we may live.

The well-fed evangels,
        the narrow-lipped and bright-eyed nuns,
                the tall,
white-haired Anglican,
        proclaim it by their appetites
                as do I also,
chomping with my worn-out teeth:
        the Lord is my shepherd
                I shall not want.

No matter how well they are fed,
        how daintily
                they put the food to their lips,
it is all
        according to the imagination!
Only the imagination
        is real! They have imagined it,

                    therefore it is so:
of the evangels,
                with the long legs characteristic of the race—
                    only the docile women
of the party smiled at me
                when, with my eyes
                    I accosted them.
The nuns—but after all
                I saw only a face, a young face
                    cut off at the brows.
It was a simple story.
                The cleric, plainly
                    from a good school,
interested me more,
                a man with whom I might
                    carry on a conversation.

No one was there
                save only for
                    the food. Which I alone,
being a poet,
                could have given them.
                    But I
had only my eyes
                with which to speak.

Deep Religious Faith

Past death
        past rainy days
                or the distraction
of lady's-smocks all silver-white;
        beyond the remote borders
                of poetry itself
if it does not drive us,
        it is vain.
                Yet it is
that which made El Greco
        paint his green and distorted saints
                and live
lean.
        It is what in life drives us
                to praise music
and the old
        or sit by a friend
                in his last hours.

All that which makes the pear ripen
        or the poet's line
                come true!
Invention is the heart of it.

Without the quirks
        and oddnesses of invention
                the paralytic is confirmed
in his paralysis,
        it is from a northern
                and half-savage country
where the religion
        is hate.

                        There
the citizens are imprisoned.
                        The rose

                                may not be worshipped
or the poet look to it
                for benefit.

In the night a
                storm of gale proportions came
                up.

                                No one was there to envisage
a field of daisies!
                There were bellowings
                                and roarings
from a child's book
                of fairy tales,
                                the rumble
of a distant bombing
                —or of a bee!
                                Shame on our poets,
they have caught the prevalent fever:
                impressed
                                by the "laboratory,"
they have forgot
                the flower!
                                which goes beyond all
laboratories!
                They have quit the job
                of invention. The
imagination has fallen asleep
                in a poppy-cup.

The Mental Hospital Garden

It is far to Assisi,
            but not too far:
                        Over this garden,
brooding over this garden,
            there is a kindly spirit,
                        brother to the poor
and who is poorer than he
            who is in love
                        when birds are nesting
in the spring of the year?
            They came
                        to eat from his hand
who had nothing,
            and yet
                        from his plenty
he fed them all.
            All mankind
                        grew to be his debtors,
a simple story.
            Love is in season.

At such a time,
            hyacinth time
                        in
the hospital garden,
            the time
                        of the coral-flowered
and early salmon-pink
            clusters, it is
                        the time also of
abandoned birds' nests
            before
                        the sparrows start
                        to tear them apart

against the advent of that bounty
                from which
                                they will build anew.

All about them
                on the lawns
                                the young couples
embrace   .
                as in a tale
                                by Boccaccio.
They are careless
                under license of the disease
                                which has restricted them
to these grounds.
                St. Francis forgive them
                                and all lovers
whoever they may be.
                They have seen
                                a great light, it
springs from their own bawdy foreheads.
                The light
                                is sequestered there
by these enclosing walls.
                They are divided
                                from their fellows.
It is a bounty
                from a last year's bird's nest.
                                St. Francis,
who befriended the wild birds,
                by their aid,
                                those who
have nothing
                and live
                                by the Holy light of love
that rules,
                blocking despair,
                                over this garden.

Time passes.
The pace has slackened
But with the falling off
of the pace
the scene has altered.
The lovers raise their heads,
at that which has come over them.
It is summer now.
The broad sun
shines!
Blinded by the light
they walk bewildered,
seeking
between the leaves
for a vantage
from which to view
the advancing season.
They are incredulous
of their own cure
and half minded
to escape
into the dark again.
The scene
indeed has changed.
By St. Francis
the whole scene
has changed.
They glimpse
a surrounding sky
and the whole countryside.
Filled with terror
they seek
a familiar flower
at which to warm themselves,
but the whole field
accosts them.
They hide their eyes

            ashamed
                        before that bounty,
peering through their fingers
                timidly.
                        The saint is watching,
his eyes filled with pity.

The year is still young
                but not so young
                        as they
who face the fears
                with which
                        they are confronted.
Reawakened
                after love's first folly
                        they resemble children
roused from a long sleep.
                Summer is here,
                        right enough.
The saint
                has tactfully withdrawn.
                        One
emboldened,
                parting the leaves before her,
                        stands in the full sunlight,
alone
                shading her eyes
                        as her heart
beats wildly
                and her mind
                        drinks up
the full meaning
                of it
                        all!

The Artist

Mr. T.
            bareheaded
                        in a soiled undershirt
his hair standing out
            on all sides
                        stood on his toes
heels together
            arms gracefully
                        for the moment
curled above his head.
            Then he whirled about
                        bounded
into the air
            and with an *entrechat*
                        perfectly achieved
completed the figure.
            My mother
                        taken by surprise
where she sat
            in her invalid's chair
                        was left speechless.
Bravo! she cried at last
            and clapped her hands.
                        The man's wife
came from the kitchen:
            What goes on here? she said.
                        But the show was over.

Theocritus: Idyl I

A Version from the Greek

THYRSIS

The whisper of the wind in
            that pine tree,
                        goatherd,
is sweet as the murmur of live water;
            likewise
                        your flute notes. After Pan
you shall bear away second prize.
            And if he
                        take the goat
with the horns,
            the she-goat
                        is yours: but if
he choose the she-goat,
            the kid will fall
                        to your lot.
And the flesh of the kid
            is dainty
                        before they begin milking them.

GOATHERD

Your song is sweeter,
            shepherd,
                        than the music
of the water as it plashes
            from the high face
                        of yonder rock!
If the Muses

choose the young ewe
            you shall receive
a stall-fed lamb
            as your reward,
                        but if
they prefer the lamb
            you
                        shall have the ewe for
                        second prize.

THYRSIS

Will you not, goatherd,
            in the Nymph's name
                        take your place on this
                        sloping knoll
among the tamarisks
            and pipe for me
                        while I tend my sheep.

GOATHERD

No, shepherd,
            nothing doing;
                        it's not for us
to be heard during the noon hush.
            We dread Pan,
                        who for a fact
is stretched out somewhere,
            dog tired from the chase;
                        his mood is bitter,
anger ready at his nostrils.
            But, Thyrsis,
                        since you are good at

singing of *The Afflictions of Daphnis,*
          and have most deeply
               meditated the pastoral mode,
come here,
        let us sit down,
            under this elm
facing Priapus and the fountain fairies,
        here where the shepherds come
           to try themselves out
by the oak trees.
        Ah! may you sing
           as you sang that day
facing Chromis out of Libya,
        I will let you milk, yes,
           three times over,
a goat that is the mother of twins
        and even when
           she has sucked her kids
her milk fills
        two pails. I will give besides,
           new made, a two-eared bowl
of ivy-wood,
        rubbed with beeswax
           that smacks still
of the knife of the carver.
        Round its upper edges
           winds the ivy, ivy
flecked with yellow flowers
        and about it
           is twisted
a tendril joyful with the saffron fruit.
        Within,
           is limned a girl,
as fair a thing as the gods have made,
        dressed in a sweeping
           gown.

Her hair
        is confined by a snood.
           Beside her
two fair-haired youths
        with alternate speech
           are contending
but her heart is
        untouched.
           Now,
she glances at one,
        smiling,
           and now, lightly
she flings the other a thought,
        while their eyes,
           by reason of love's
long vigils, are heavy
        but their labors
           all in vain.
In addition
        there is fashioned there
           an ancient fisherman
and a rock,
        a rugged rock,
           on which
with might and main
        the old man poises a great net
           for the cast
as one who puts his whole heart into it.
        One would say
           that he was fishing
with the full strength of his limbs
        so big do his muscles stand out
           about the neck.
Gray-haired though he be,
        he has the strength
           of a young man.

Now, separated
            from the sea-broken old man
                        by a narrow interval
is a vineyard,
            heavy
                        with fire-red clusters,
and on a rude wall
            sits a small boy
                        guarding them.
Round him
            two she-foxes are skulking.
                        One
goes the length of the vine-rows
            to eat the grapes
                        while the other
brings all her cunning to bear,
            by what has been set down,
                        vowing
she will never quit the lad
            until
                        she leaves him bare
and breakfastless.
            But the boy
                        is plaiting a pretty
cage of locust stalks and asphodel,
            fitting in the reeds
                        and cares less for his scrip
and the vines
            than he takes delight
                        in his plaiting.
All about the cup
            is draped the mild acanthus
                        a miracle of varied work,
a thing for you to marvel at.
            I paid
                        a Caledonian ferryman

a goat and a great white
                cream-cheese
                                for the bowl.
It is still virgin to me,
                its lip has never touched mine.
                                To gain my desire,
I would gladly
                give this cup
                                if you, my friend,
will sing for me
                that delightful song.
                                I hold nothing back.
Begin, my friend,
                for you cannot,
                                you may be sure,
take your song,
                which drives all things out of mind,
                                with you to the other world.

The Desert Music

–the dance begins: to end about a form
propped motionless—on the bridge
between Juárez and El Paso—unrecognizable
in the semi-dark

                    Wait!

The others waited while you inspected it,
on the very walk itself

                    Is it alive?

                              —neither a head,
legs nor arms!

            It isn't a sack of rags someone
has abandoned here   torpid against
the flange of the supporting girder   ?

                    an inhuman shapelessness,
knees hugged tight up into the belly

        Egg-shaped!

                    What a place to sleep!
on the International Boundary.   Where else,
interjurisdictional, not to be disturbed?

How shall we get said what must be said?

Only the poem.

Only the counted poem, to an exact measure:
to imitate, not to copy nature, not
to copy nature

NOT, prostrate, to copy nature
                            but a dance! to dance
two and two with him—
                    sequestered there asleep,
                              right end up!

    A music
supersedes his composure, hallooing to us
across a great distance   .   .

                              wakens the dance
who blows upon his benumbed fingers!

                        Only the poem
only the made poem, to get said what must
be said, not to copy nature, sticks
in our throats   .

The law?   The law gives us nothing
but a corpse, wrapped in a dirty mantle.
The law is based on murder and confinement,
long delayed,
but this, following the insensate music,
is based on the dance:

                    an agony of self-realization
bound into a whole
by that which surrounds us   .

                        I cannot escape

I cannot vomit it up

Only the poem!

Only the made poem, the verb calls it
                              into being.

                    —it looks too small for a man.
A woman.   Or a very shriveled old man.
Maybe dead.   They probably inspect the place
and will cart it away later   .

                    Heave it into the river.
A good thing.

Leaving California to return east, the fertile desert,
                    (were it to get water)
surrounded us, a music of survival, subdued, distant, half
                    heard; we were engulfed
by it as in the early evening, seeing the wind lift
                    and drive the sand, we
passed Yuma. All night long, heading for El Paso to
                    meet our friend,
we slept fitfully.   Thinking of Paris, I waked to the tick
                    of the rails.   The
jagged desert   .

                              —to tell
what subsequently I saw and what heard

                              —to place myself (in
my nature) beside nature

                    —to imitate
nature (for to copy nature would be a
        shameful thing)

                    I lay myself down:

The Old Market's a good place to begin:
Let's cut through here—
                              tequila's only
a nickel a slug in these side streets.
Keep out though.   Oh, it's all right at
this time of day but I saw H. terribly
beaten up in one of those joints.   He
asked for it.   I thought he was going to
be killed.   I do
my drinking on the main drag   .

                         That's the bull ring
Oh, said Floss, after she got used to the
change of light   .
                         What color!   Isn't it
wonderful!

         —paper flowers (*para los santos*)
baked red-clay utensils, daubed
with blue, silverware,
dried peppers, onions, print goods, children's
clothing   .   the place deserted all but
for a few Indians squatted in the
booths, unnoticing (don't you think it)
as though they slept there   .

         There's a second tier.   Do you
want to go up?

         What makes Texans so tall?
We saw a woman this morning in a mink cape
six feet if she was an inch.   What a woman!

Probably a Broadway figure.

—tell you what else we saw: about a million
sparrows screaming their heads off

in the trees of that small park where
the buses stop, sanctuary,
I suppose,
from the wind driving the sand in that way
about the city   .

                             Texas rain they call it

—and those two alligators in the fountain   .

There were four

                 I saw only two

                          They were looking
right at you all the time   .

Penny please!   Give me penny please, mister.

                  Don't give them anything.

                        .   instinctively
one has already drawn one's naked
wrist away from those obscene fingers
as in the mind a vague apprehension speaks
and the music rouses   .

                     Let's get in here.
             a music!   cut off as
the bar door closes behind us.

             We've got
another half hour.

             —returned to the street,
the pressure moves from booth to booth along

the curb.   Opposite, no less insistent
the better stores are wide open.   Come in
and look around.   You don't have to buy: hats,
riding boots, blankets   .

                Look at the way,
slung from her neck with a shawl, that young
Indian woman carries her baby!

                —a stream of Spanish,
as she brushes by, intense, wide-
eyed in eager talk with her boy husband

—three half-grown girls, one of them eating a
pomegranate.   Laughing.

                   and the serious tourist,
man and wife, middle-aged, middle-western,
their arms loaded with loot, whispering
together—still looking for bargains   .

                  and the aniline
red and green candy at the little booth
tended by the old Indian woman.
        Do you suppose anyone actually
buys—and eats the stuff?

My feet are beginning to ache me.

                We still got a few minutes.
Let's try here.   They had the mayor
up last month for taking $3000 a week from
the whorehouses of the city.   Not much left
for the girls.   There's a show on.

             Only a few tables
occupied.   A conventional orchestra—this

place livens up later—playing the usual local
jing-a-jing—a boy and girl team, she
                          confidential with someone
off stage.   Laughing: just finishing the act.

So we drink until the next turn—a strip tease.

Do you mean it?   Wow!   Look at her.

                          You'd have to be
pretty drunk to get any kick out of that.
She's no Mexican.   Some worn-out trouper from
the States.   Look at those breasts   .

            There is a fascination
            seeing her shake
            the beaded sequins from
            a string about her hips

            She gyrates but it's
            not what you think,
            one does not laugh
            to watch her belly.

            One is moved but not
            at the dull show.   The
            guitarist yawns.   She
            cannot even sing.   She

            has about her painted
            hardihood a screen
            of pretty doves which
            flutter their wings.

            Her cold eyes perfunc-
            torily moan but do not

smile.   Yet they bill
and coo by grace of
a certain candor.   She

is heavy on her feet.
That's good.   She
bends forward leaning
on the table of the
balding man sitting
upright, alone, so that
everything hangs for-
ward.
     What the hell
are you grinning
to yourself about?   Not
at *her?*
     The music!
I like her.   She fits

the music   .

Why don't these Indians get over this nauseating
prattle about their souls and their loves and sing
us something else for a change?

This place is rank
with it.   She
at least knows she's
part of another tune,
knows her customers,
has the same
opinion of them as I
have.   That gives her
one up   .   one up
following the lying
music   .

There is another music.   The bright-colored candy
of her nakedness lifts her unexpectedly
to partake of its tune   .

                              Andromeda of those rocks,
the virgin of her mind   .   those unearthly
greens and reds

                              in her mockery of virtue
she becomes unaccountably virtuous   .
                              though she in no
way pretends it   .

Let's get out of this.

                              In the street it hit
me in the face as we started to walk again.   Or
am I merely playing the poet?   Do I merely invent
it out of whole cloth?   I thought   .

                    What in the form of an old whore in
                    a cheap Mexican joint in Juárez, her bare
                    can waggling crazily can be
                    so refreshing to me, raise to my ear
                    so sweet a tune, built of such slime?

                    Here we are. They'll be along any minute.
                    The bar is at the right of the entrance,
                    a few tables opposite which you have to pass
                    to get to the dining room, beyond.

                    A foursome, two oversize Americans, no
                    longer young, got up as cowboys,
                    hats and all, are drunk and carrying on
                    with their gals, drunk also,

                    especially one inciting her man, the
                    biggest, *Yip ee*! to dance in

the narrow space, oblivious to everything
—she is insatiable and he is trying

stumblingly to keep up with her.
Give it the gun, pardner! *Yip ee*! We
pushed by them to our table, seven
of us.   Seated about the room

were quiet family groups, some with
children, eating.   Rather a better
class than you notice
on the streets.   So here we are.   You

can see through into the kitchen
where one of the cooks, his shirt sleeves
rolled up, an apron over
the well-pressed pants of a street

suit, black hair neatly parted,
a tall
good-looking man, is working
absorbed, before a chopping block

Old fashioneds all around?

So this is William
Carlos Williams, the poet   .

Floss and I had half consumed
our quartered hearts of lettuce before
we noticed the others hadn't touched theirs   .
You seem quite normal.   Can you tell me?   Why
does one want to write a poem?

Because it's there to be written.

Oh.   A matter of inspiration then?

                                    Of necessity.
Oh.   But what sets it off?

                    I am that he whose brains
                    are scattered
                              aimlessly

                              —and so,
the hour done, the quail eaten, we were on
our way back to El Paso.

                              Good night.   Good
night and thank you   . No. Thank you. We're
going to walk   .

—and so, on the naked wrist, we feel again
those insistent fingers   .

                              Penny please, mister.
Penny please.   Give me penny.

                              Here! now go away.

—but the music, the music has reawakened
as we leave the busier parts of the street
and come again to the bridge in the semi-dark,
pay our fee and begin again to cross   .
seeing the lights along the mountain back of El
Paso and pause to watch the boys calling out
to us to throw more coins to them standing
in the shallow water   .   so that's
where the incentive lay, with the annoyance
of those surprising fingers.

                              So you're a poet?
a good thing to be got rid of—half drunk,

a free dinner under your belt, even though you
get typhoid—and to have met people you
can at least talk to   .

            relief from that changeless, endless
inescapable and insistent music   .

            What else, Latins, do you yourselves
seek but relief!
with the expressionless ding dong you dish up
to us of your souls and your loves, which
we swallow. Spaniards! (though these are mostly
Indians who chase the white bastards
through the streets on their Independence Day
and try to kill them)   .

                      What's that?

Oh, come on.

            But what's THAT?

                the music! the
music! as when Casals struck
and held a deep cello tone
and I am speechless   .

                  There it sat
in the projecting angle of the bridge flange
as I stood aghast and looked at it—
in the half-light: shapeless or rather returned
to its original shape, armless, legless,
headless, packed like the pit of a fruit into
that obscure corner—or
a fish to swim against the stream—or
a child in the womb prepared to imitate life,

warding its life against
a birth of awful promise.   The music
guards it, a mucus, a film that surrounds it,
a benumbing ink that stains the
sea of our minds—to hold us off—shed
of a shape close as it can get to no shape,
a music! a protecting music   .

                              I *am* a poet! I
am.   I am.   I am a poet, I reaffirmed, ashamed

Now the music volleys through as in
a lonely moment I hear it.   Now it is all
about me.   The dance!   The verb detaches itself
seeking to become articulate   .

                    And I could not help thinking
                    of the wonders of the brain that
                    hears that music and of our
                    skill sometimes to record it.

Journey to Love

(1955)

For My Wife

A Negro Woman

carrying a bunch of marigolds
        wrapped
                in an old newspaper:
She carries them upright,
        bareheaded,
                the bulk
of her thighs
        causing her to waddle
                as she walks
looking into
        the store window which she passes
                on her way.
What is she
        but an ambassador
                from another world
a world of pretty marigolds
        of two shades
                which she announces
not knowing what she does
        other
                than walk the streets
holding the flowers upright
        as a torch
                so early in the morning.

The Ivy Crown

The whole process is a lie,
    unless,
        crowned by excess,
it break forcefully,
    one way or another,
        from its confinement—
or find a deeper well.
    Antony and Cleopatra
        were right;
they have shown
    the way. I love you
        or I do not live
at all.

Daffodil time
    is past. This is
        summer, summer!
the heart says,
    and not even the full of it.
        No doubts
are permitted—
    though they will come
        and may
before our time
    overwhelm us.
        We are only mortal
but being mortal
    can defy our fate.
        We may
by an outside chance
    even win! We do not
        look to see
jonquils and violets

                come again
                        but there are,
still,
                the roses!

Romance has no part in it.
                The business of love is
                        cruelty *which*,
by our wills,
                we transform
                        to live together.
It has its seasons,
                for and against,
                        whatever the heart
fumbles in the dark
                to assert
                        toward the end of May.
Just as the nature of briars
                is to tear flesh,
                        I have proceeded
through them.
                Keep
                        the briars out,
they say.
                You cannot live
                        and keep free of
briars.

Children pick flowers.
                Let them.
                        Though having them
in hand
                they have no further use for them
                        but leave them crumpled
at the curb's edge.

At our age the imagination
                across the sorry facts
                                lifts us
to make roses
                stand before thorns.
                                Sure
love is cruel
                and selfish
                                and totally obtuse—
at least, blinded by the light,
                young love is.
                                But we are older,
I to love
                and you to be loved,
                                we have,
no matter how,
                by our wills survived
                                to keep
the jeweled prize
                always
                                at our finger tips.
We will it so
                and so it is
                                past all accident.

View by Color Photography
on a Commercial Calendar

The church of Vice-Morcate
            in the Canton Ticino
                        with its apple blossoms
is beautiful
            as anything I have ever seen
                        in or out of
Switzerland.
            The beauty of holiness
                        the beauty of a man's anger
reflecting his sex
            or a woman's either,
                        mountainous,
or a little stone church
            from a height
                        or
close to the camera
            the apple tree in blossom
                        or the far lake
below
            in the distance—
                        are equal
as they are unsurpassed.
            Peace
                        after the event
comes from their contemplation,
            a great peace.
                        The sky is cut off,
there is no horizon
            just the mountainside
                        bordered by water
on which tiny waves

                without passion
                            unconcerned
    cover the invisible fish.
                And who but we are concerned
                            with the beauty of apple blossoms
    and a small church
                on a promontory,
                            an ancient church—
    by the look of its masonry—
                abandoned
                            by a calm lake
    in the mountains
                where the sun shines
                            of a springtime
    afternoon. Something
                has come to an end here,
                            it has been accomplished.

The Sparrow

(To My Father)

This sparrow
        who comes to sit at my window
                is a poetic truth
more than a natural one.
        His voice,
                his movements,
his habits—
        how he loves to
                flutter his wings
in the dust—
        all attest it;
                granted, he does it
to rid himself of lice
        but the relief he feels
                makes him
cry out lustily—
        which is a trait
                more related to music
than otherwise.
        Wherever he finds himself
                in early spring,
on back streets
        or beside palaces,
                he carries on
unaffectedly
        his amours.
                It begins in the egg,
his sex genders it:
        What is more pretentiously
                useless
or about which
        we more pride ourselves?

It leads as often as not
to our undoing.
The cockerel, the crow
with their challenging voices
cannot surpass
the insistence
of his cheep!
Once
at El Paso
toward evening,
I saw—and heard!—
ten thousand sparrows
who had come in from
the desert
to roost. They filled the trees
of a small park. Men fled
(with ears ringing!)
from their droppings,
leaving the premises
to the alligators
who inhabit
the fountain. His image
is familiar
as that of the aristocratic
unicorn, a pity
there are not more oats eaten
nowadays
to make living easier
for him.
At that,
his small size,
keen eyes,
serviceable beak
and general truculence
assure his survival—
to say nothing
of his innumerable

brood.
> Even the Japanese
> > know him
and have painted him
> sympathetically,
> > with profound insight
into his minor
> characteristics.
> > Nothing even remotely
subtle
> about his lovemaking.
> > He crouches
before the female,
> drags his wings,
> > waltzing,
throws back his head
> and simply—
> > yells! The din
is terrific.
> The way he swipes his bill
> > across a plank
to clean it,
> is decisive.
> > So with everything
he does. His coppery
> eyebrows
> > give him the air
of being always
> a winner—and yet
> > I saw once,
the female of his species
> clinging determinedly
> > to the edge of
a water pipe,
> catch him
> > by his crown-feathers
to hold him   •

                    silent,
                              subdued,
hanging above the city streets
                    until
                              she was through with him.
What was the use
          of that?
                              She hung there
herself,
                    puzzled at her success.
                              I laughed heartily.
Practical to the end,
          it is the poem
                    of his existence
that triumphed
          finally;
                              a wisp of feathers
flattened to the pavement,
                    wings spread symmetrically
                              as if in flight,
the head gone,
                    the black escutcheon of the breast
                              undecipherable,
an effigy of a sparrow,
          a dried wafer only,
                              left to say
and it says it
          without offense,
                              beautifully;
This was I,
          a sparrow.
                              I did my best;
farewell.

The King!

Nell Gwyn,
        it says in the dictionary,
                actress
and mistress of Charles the Second:
        what a lot
                of pious rot there is
surrounding
        that
                simple statement.
She waked in the morning,
        bathed in
                the King's bountiful
water
        which enveloped her
                completely and,
magically,
        with the grit, took away
                all her sins.
It was the King's body
        which was served;
                the King's boards which
in the evening
        she capably trod;
                she fed
the King's poor
        and when she died,
                left them some slight moneys
under certain
        conditions.

Happy the woman
        whose husband makes her
                the "King's whore."
All this you will find

in the dictionary
                     where it has been
preserved forever—
                  since it is beautiful
                                 and true.

The Lady Speaks

A storm raged among the live oaks
                  while my husband and I
                                 sat in the semi-dark
listening!
                  We watched from the windows,
                                 the lights off,
saw the moss
                  whipped upright
                                 by the wind's force.
Two candles we had lit
                  side by side
                                 before us
so solidly had our house been built
                  kept their tall flames
                                 unmoved.
May it be so
                  when a storm sends the moss
                                 whipping
back and forth
                  upright
                                 above my head
like flames in the final
                  fury.

Tribute to the Painters

Satyrs dance!
                all the deformities take wing
                        centaurs
leading to the rout of the vocables
                in the writings
of Gertrude
            Stein—but
                        you cannot be
an artist
            by mere ineptitude
The dream
            is in pursuit!

The neat figures of
            Paul Klee
                        fill the canvas
but that
            is not the work
                        of a child
The cure began, perhaps,
            with the abstractions
                        of Arabic art
Dürer
            with his *Melancholy*
                        was ware of it—
the shattered masonry. Leonardo
            saw it,
                        the obsession,
and ridiculed it
            in *La Gioconda*.
                        Bosch's
congeries of tortured souls and devils
            who prey on them
                        fish

swallowing
       their own entrails
Freud
       Picasso
             Juan Gris.
The letter from a friend
       saying:
             For the last
three nights
       I have slept like a baby
             without
liquor or dope of any sort!
       We know
             that a stasis
from a chrysalis
       has stretched its wings—
             like a bull
or the Minotaur
       or Beethoven
             in the scherzo
of his 9th Symphony
       stomped
             his heavy feet
I saw love
       mounted naked on a horse
             on a swan
the back of a fish
       the bloodthirsty conger eel
             and laughed
recalling the Jew
       in the pit
             among his fellows
when the indifferent chap
       with the machine gun
             was spraying the heap.

He
              had not yet been hit
                        but smiled
comforting his companions.

Dreams possess me
              and the dance
                        of my thoughts
involving animals
              the blameless beasts
and there came to me
              just now
                        the knowledge of
the tyranny of the image
              and how
                        men
in their designs
              have learned
                        to shatter it
whatever it may be,
              that the trouble
                        in their minds
shall be quieted,
              put to bed
                        again.

To a Man Dying on His Feet

    —not that we are not all
           "dying on our feet"
                but the look you give me
and to which I bow,
           is more immediate.
                It is keenly alert,
suspicious of me—
           as of all that are living—and
                apologetic.
Your jaw
           wears the stubble
                of a haggard beard,
a dirty beard,
           which resembles
                the snow through which
your long legs
           are conducting you.
                Whither? Where are you going?
This would be a fine day
           to go on a journey.
                Say to Florida
where at this season
           all go
                nowadays.
There grows the hibiscus,
           the star jasmine
                and more than I can tell
but the odors
           from what I know
                must be alluring.
Come with me there!
           you look like a good guy,
                come this evening.

The plane leaves at 6:30
        or have you another
                appointment?

Come on!

A different kind of thought
        blander
                and more desperate
like that of
        Sergeant So-and-So
            at the road
in Belleau Wood:
        Come on!
            Do you want to live
forever?—
        That
            is the essence
of poetry.
        But it does not
            always
take the same form.
        For the most part
            it consists
in listening
        to the nightingale
            or fools.

The Pink Locust

I'm persistent as the pink locust,
            once admitted
                        to the garden,
you will not easily get rid of it.
            Tear it from the ground,
                        if one hair-thin rootlet
remain
            it will come again.
                        It is
flattering to think of myself
            so. It is also
                        laughable.
A modest flower,
            resembling a pink sweet-pea,
                        you cannot help
but admire it
            until its habits
                        become known.
Are we not most of us
            like that? It would be
                        too much
if the public
            pried among the minutiae
                        of our private affairs.
Not
            that we have anything to hide
                        but could *they*
stand it? Of course
            the world would be gratified
                        to find out
what fools we have made of ourselves.
            The question is,
                        would they

140

be generous with us—
              as we have been
                        with others? It is,
as I say,
         a flower
                  incredibly resilient
under attack!
              Neglect it
                        and it will grow into a tree.
I wish I could *so* think of myself
              and of what
                        is to become of me.
The poet himself,
              what does he think of himself
                        facing his world?
It will not do to say,
              as he is inclined to say:
                        Not much. The poem
would be in *that* betrayed.
              He might as well answer—
                        "a rose is a rose
is a rose" and let it go at that.
              A rose *is* a rose
                        and the poem equals it
if it be well made.
              The poet
                        cannot slight himself
without slighting
              his poem—
                        which would be
ridiculous.
              Life offers
                        no greater reward.
And so,
        like this flower,
                  I persist—

for what there may be in it.
                I am not,
                                I know,
in the galaxy of poets
                a rose
                                but *who*, among the rest,
will deny me
                my place.

Classic Picture

It is a classic picture,
                women have always fussed with their hair
                                (having no sisters
I never watched the process
                so intimately
                                as this time); the reason for it
is not clear—
                tho' I acknowledge,
                                an unkempt head of hair,
while not as repulsive as a nest of snakes,
                is repulsive enough
                                in a woman.
Therefore
                she fusses with her hair
                                for
a woman does not want to seem repulsive,
                unless
                                to gain for herself

she be hungry,
          hungry!
                    as would be a man
and all hunger is repulsive
          and puts on
                    an ugly face.
Their heads are not made as a man's,
          an ornament
                    in itself. They have
other charms—
          needless
                    to enumerate. Under
their ornate coiffures
          lurks a specter,
                    coiling snakes
doubling for tresses

A woman's brains
          which can be keen
                    are condemned,
like a poet's,
          to what deceptions she can muster
                    to lead men
to their ruin.
          But look more deeply
                    into her maneuvers,
and puzzle as we will about them
          they may mean
                    anything

Address:

To a look in my son's eyes—
       I hope he did not see
              that I was looking—
that I have seen
       often enough
              in the mirror,
a male look
       approaching despair—
              there is a female look
to match it
       no need to speak of that:
              Perhaps
it was only a dreamy look
       not an unhappy one
              but absent
from the world—
       such as plagued the eyes
              of Bobby Burns
in his youth and threw him
       into the arms
              of women—
in which he could
       forget himself,
              not defiantly,
but with full acceptance
       of his lot
              as a man
His Jean forgave him
       and took him to her heart
              time after time
when he would be
       too drunk
              with Scotch

or the love of other women
        to notice
                what he was doing.
What was he intent upon
        but to drown out
                that look? What
does it portend?
        A war
                will not erase it
nor a bank account,
        estlin,
                amounting to 9 figures.
Flow gently sweet Afton
        among thy green braes—
                no matter
that he wrote the song
        to another woman
                it was never for sale.

The Drunk and the Sailor

The petty fury
           that disrupts my life—
                       at the striking of a wrong key
as if it had been
           a woman lost
or a fortune   .   .
               The man was obviously drunk,
                       Christopher Marlowe
could have been no drunker
               when he got himself
                       stuck through the eye
with a poniard.
               The bus station was crowded.
The man
           heavy-set
                       about my own age
seventy
           was talking privately
                       with a sailor.
He had an ugly jaw on him.
           Suddenly
                       sitting there on the bench
too drunk to stand
           he began menacingly
                       his screaming.
The young sailor
           who could have flattened him
                       at one blow
kept merely looking at him.
               The nerve-tingling screeches
                       that sprang
sforzando
           from that stubble beard

     would have distinguished
an operatic tenor.
    But me—
       the shock of it—
my heart leaped in my chest
    so that I saw red
       wanted
to strangle the guy
     The fury of love
       is no less.

A Smiling Dane

The Danish native
              before the Christian era
                          whose body
features intact
              with a rope
                          also intact
round the neck
              found recently
                          in a peat bog
is dead.
                    Are you surprised?
                          You should be.
The diggers
              who discovered him
                          expected more.
Frightened
              they quit the place
                          thinking
his ghost might walk.

The cast of his features
              shows him
                          to be
a man of intelligence.
              It did him no good.
                          What his eyes saw
cannot be more
              than the male
                          and female
of it—
              if as much.
                          His stomach
its contents examined
              shows him
                          before he died

to have had
          a meal
                    consisting of local grains
swallowed whole
          which he probably enjoyed
                    though he did not
much as we do
          chew them.
                    And what if
the image of his frightened executioners
          is not recorded?
                    Do we not know
their features
          as if
                    it had occurred
today?
          We can still see in his smile
                    their grimaces.

Shadows

Shadows cast by the street light
        under the stars,
                the head is tilted back,
the long shadow of the legs
        presumes a world
                taken for granted
on which the cricket trills.
        The hollows of the eyes
                are unpeopled.
Right and left
        climb the ladders of night
                as dawn races
to put out the stars.
        That
                is the poetic figure
but we know
        better: what is not now
                will never
be. Sleep secure,
        the little dog in the snapshot
                keeps his shrewd eyes
pared. Memory
        is liver than sight.
                A man
looking out,
        seeing the shadows—
                it is himself
that can be painlessly amputated
        by a mere shifting
                of the stars.
A comfort so easily not to be

and to be at once one
                with every man.
The night blossoms
            with a thousand shadows
                    so long
as there are stars,
            street lights
                    or a moon and
who shall say
            by their shadows
which is different
            from the other
                    fat or lean.

II

Ripped from the concept of our lives
            and from all concept
                    somehow, and plainly,
the sun will come up
            each morning
                    and sink again.
So that we experience
            violently
                    every day
two worlds
            one of which we share with the
            rose in bloom
                    and one,
by far the greater,
            with the past,
                    the world of memory,
the silly world of history,
            the world
                    of the imagination.

Which leaves only the beasts and trees,
                crystals
                        with their refractive
                        surfaces
and rotting things
                to stir our wonder.
                        Save for the little
central hole
                of the eye itself
                        into which
we dare not stare too hard
                or we are lost.
                        The instant
trivial as it is
                is all we have
                        unless—unless
things the imagination feeds upon,
                the scent of the rose,
                        startle us anew.

Asphodel, That Greeny Flower

BOOK I

Of asphodel, that greeny flower,
        like a buttercup
                upon its branching stem—
save that it's green and wooden—
        I come, my sweet,
                to sing to you.
We lived long together
        a life filled,
                if you will,
with flowers. So that
        I was cheered
                when I came first to know
that there were flowers also
        in hell.
                Today
I'm filled with the fading memory of those flowers
        that we both loved,
                even to this poor
colorless thing—
        I saw it
                when I was a child—
little prized among the living
        but the dead see,
                asking among themselves:
What do I remember
        that was shaped
                as this thing is shaped?
while our eyes fill
        with tears.
                Of love, abiding love
it will be telling

                though too weak a wash of crimson
                            colors it
        to make it wholly credible.
                There is something
                            something urgent
        I have to say to you
                    and you alone
                            but it must wait
        while I drink in
                the joy of your approach,
                            perhaps for the last time.
        And so
                    with fear in my heart
                            I drag it out
        and keep on talking
                for I dare not stop.
                            Listen while I talk on
        against time.
                    It will not be
                            for long.
        I have forgot
                and yet I see clearly enough
                            something
        central to the sky
                which ranges round it.
                            An odor
        springs from it!
                    A sweetest odor!
                            Honeysuckle! And now
        there comes the buzzing of a bee!
                and a whole flood
                            of sister memories!
        Only give me time,
                    time to recall them
                            before I shall speak out.
        Give me time,
                    time.

When I was a boy
        I kept a book
                to which, from time
to time,
        I added pressed flowers
                until, after a time,
I had a good collection.
        The asphodel,
                forebodingly,
among them.
        I bring you,
                reawakened,
a memory of those flowers.
        They were sweet
                when I pressed them
and retained
        something of their sweetness
                a long time.
It is a curious odor,
        a moral odor,
                that brings me
near to you.
        The color
                was the first to go.
There had come to me
        a challenge,
                your dear self,
mortal as I was,
        the lily's throat
                to the hummingbird!
Endless wealth,
        I thought,
                held out its arms to me.
A thousand topics
        in an apple blossom.
                The generous earth itself

155

gave us lief.
         The whole world
                  became my garden!
But the sea
         which no one tends
                  is also a garden
when the sun strikes it
         and the waves
                  are wakened.
I have seen it
         and so have you
                  when it puts all flowers
to shame.
         Too, there are the starfish
                  stiffened by the sun
and other sea wrack
         and weeds. We knew that
                  along with the rest of it
for we were born by the sea,
         knew its rose hedges
                  to the very water's brink.
There the pink mallow grows
         and in their season
                  strawberries
and there, later,
         we went to gather
                  the wild plum.
I cannot say
         that I have gone to hell
                  for your love
but often
         found myself there
                  in your pursuit.
I do not like it
         and wanted to be
                  in heaven. Hear me out.

Do not turn away.

I have learned much in my life
                from books
                                and out of them
about love.
                Death
                                is not the end of it.
There is a hierarchy
                which can be attained,
                                I think,
in its service.
                Its guerdon
                                is a fairy flower;
a cat of twenty lives.
                If no one came to try it
                                the world
would be the loser.
                It has been
                                for you and me
as one who watches a storm
                come in over the water.
                                We have stood
from year to year
                before the spectacle of our lives
                                with joined hands.
The storm unfolds.
                Lightning
                                plays about the edges of the clouds.
The sky to the north
                is placid,
                                blue in the afterglow
as the storm piles up.
                It is a flower
                                that will soon reach
the apex of its bloom.
                We danced,

in our minds,
and read a book together.
                You remember?
                        It was a serious book.
And so books
            entered our lives.
The sea! The sea!
            Always
                    when I think of the sea
there comes to mind
        the *Iliad*
                    and Helen's public fault
that bred it.
            Were it not for that
                        there would have been
no poem but the world
            if we had remembered,
                    those crimson petals
spilled among the stones,
            would have called it simply
                    murder.
The sexual orchid that bloomed then
            sending so many
                    disinterested
men to their graves
        has left its memory
                    to a race of fools
or heroes
        if silence is a virtue.
                    The sea alone
with its multiplicity
            holds any hope.
                    The storm
has proven abortive
        but we remain
                    after the thoughts it roused

to
        re-cement our lives.
               It is the mind
the mind
        that must be cured
              short of death's
intervention,
        and the will becomes again
              a garden. The poem
is complex and the place made
        in our lives
              for the poem.
Silence can be complex too,
        but you do not get far
              with silence.
Begin again.
        It is like Homer's
              catalogue of ships:
it fills up the time.
        I speak in figures,
              well enough, the dresses
you wear are figures also,
        we could not meet
              otherwise. When I speak
of flowers
        it is to recall
              that at one time
we were young.
        All women are not Helen,
              I know that,
but have Helen in their hearts.
        My sweet,
              you have it also, therefore
I love you
        and could not love you otherwise.
              Imagine you saw

a field made up of women
all silver-white.
What should you do
but love them?
The storm bursts
or fades! it is not
the end of the world.
Love is something else,
or so I thought it,
a garden which expands,
though I knew you as a woman
and never thought otherwise,
until the whole sea
has been taken up
and all its gardens.
It was the love of love,
the love that swallows up all else,
a grateful love,
a love of nature, of people,
animals,
a love engendering
gentleness and goodness
that moved me
and *that* I saw in you.
I should have known
though I did not,
that the lily-of-the-valley
is a flower makes many ill
who whiff it.
We had our children,
rivals in the general onslaught.
I put them aside
though I cared for them
as well as any man
could care for his children
according to my lights.

You understand
           I had to meet you
                    after the event
and have still to meet you.
           Love
                    to which you too shall bow
along with me—
           a flower
                    a weakest flower
shall be our trust
           and not because
                    we are too feeble
to do otherwise
           but because
                    at the height of my power
I risked what I had to do,
           therefore to prove
                    that we love each other
while my very bones sweated
           that I could not cry to you
                    in the act.
Of asphodel, that greeny flower,
           I come, my sweet,
                    to sing to you!
My heart rouses
           thinking to bring you news
                    of something
that concerns you
           and concerns many men. Look at
                    what passes for the new.
You will not find it there but in
           despised poems.
                    It is difficult
to get the news from poems
           yet men die miserably every day
                    for lack

161

of what is found there.
                  Hear me out
                          for I too am concerned
and every man
            who wants to die at peace in his bed
                          besides.

BOOK II

Approaching death,
            as we think, the death of love,
                          no distinction
any more suffices to differentiate
            the particulars
                          of place and condition
with which we have been long
            familiar.
                          All appears
as if seen
            wavering through water.
                          We start awake with a cry
of recognition
            but soon the outlines
                          become again vague.
If we are to understand our time,
            we must find the key to it,
                          not in the eighteenth
and nineteenth centuries,
            but in earlier, wilder
                          and darker epochs .   .
So to know, what I have to know
            about my own death,
                          if it be real,

I have to take it apart.
What does your generation think
of Cézanne?
I asked a young artist.
The abstractions of Hindu painting,
he replied,
is all at the moment which interests me.
He liked my poem
about the parts
of a broken bottle,
lying green in the cinders
of a hospital courtyard.
There was also, to his mind,
the one on gay wallpaper
which he had heard about
but not read.
I was grateful to him
for his interest.
Do you remember
how at Interlaken
we were waiting, four days,
to see the Jungfrau
but rain had fallen steadily.
Then
just before train time
on a tip from one of the waitresses
we rushed
to the Gipfel Platz
and there it was!
in the distance
covered with new-fallen snow.
When I was at Granada,
I remember,
in the overpowering heat
climbing a treeless hill
overlooking the Alhambra.

At my appearance at the summit
             two small boys
                         who had been playing
there
             made themselves scarce.
                         Starting to come down
by a new path
             I at once found myself surrounded
                         by gypsy women
who came up to me,
             I could speak little Spanish,
                         and directed me,
guided by a young girl,
             on my way.
                         These were the pinnacles.
The deaths I suffered
             began in the heads
                         about me, my eyes
were too keen
             not to see through
                         the world's niggardliness.
I accepted it
             as my fate.
                         The wealthy
I defied
             or not so much they,
                         for they have their uses,
as they who take their cues from them.
             I lived
                         to breathe above the stench
not knowing how I in my own person
             would be overcome
                         finally. I was lost
failing the poem.
             But if I have come from the sea
                         it is not to be

164

wholly
              fascinated by the glint of waves.
                    The free interchange
of light over their surface
          which I have compared
              to a garden
should not deceive us
          or prove
              too difficult a figure.
The poem
          if it reflects the sea
              reflects only
its dance
          upon that profound depth
              where
it seems to triumph.
          The bomb puts an end
              to all that.
I am reminded
          that the bomb
              also
is a flower
          dedicated
              howbeit
to our destruction.
          The mere picture
              of the exploding bomb
fascinates us
          so that we cannot wait
              to prostrate ourselves
before it. We do not believe
          that love
              can so wreck our lives.
The end
          will come
              in its time.

Meanwhile
        we are sick to death
                of the bomb
and its childlike
        insistence.
                Death is no answer,
no answer—
        to a blind old man
                whose bones
have the movement
        of the sea,
                a sexless old man
for whom it is a sea
        of which his verses
                are made up.
There is no power
        so great as love
                which is a sea,
which is a garden—
        as enduring
                as the verses
of that blind old man
        destined
                to live forever.
Few men believe that
        nor in the games of children.
                They believe rather
in the bomb
        and shall die by
                the bomb.
Compare Darwin's voyage of the *Beagle*,
        a voyage of discovery if there ever was one,
                to the death
incommunicado
        in the electric chair
                of the Rosenbergs.

It is the mark of the times
        that though we condemn
                what they stood for
we admire their fortitude.
        But Darwin
                opened our eyes
to the gardens of the world,
        as *they* closed them.
                Or take that other voyage
which promised so much
        but due to the world's avarice
                breeding hatred
through fear,
        ended so disastrously;
            a voyage
with which I myself am so deeply concerned,
        that of the *Pinta*,
            the *Niña*
and the *Santa María*.
        How the world opened its eyes!
            It was a flower
upon which April
        had descended from the skies!
        How bitter
a disappointment!
        In all,
            this led mainly
to the deaths I have suffered.
        For there had been kindled
            more minds
than that of the discoverers
        and set dancing
            to a measure,
a new measure!
        Soon lost.
            The measure itself

has been lost
                and we suffer for it.
                                We come to our deaths
in silence.
                The bomb speaks.
                                All suppressions,
from the witchcraft trials at Salem
                to the latest
                                book burnings
are confessions
                that the bomb
                                has entered our lives
to destroy us.
                Every drill
                                driven into the earth
for oil enters my side
                also.
                                Waste, waste!
dominates the world.
                It is the bomb's work.
                                What else was the fire
at the Jockey Club in Buenos Aires
                (*malos aires,* we should say)
                                when with Perón's connivance
the hoodlums destroyed,
                along with the books
                                the priceless Goyas
that hung there?
                You know how we treasured
                                the few paintings
we still cling to
                especially the one
                                by the dead
Charlie Demuth.
                With your smiles
                                and other trivia of the sort

my secret life
        has been made up,
                some baby's life
which had been lost
        had I not intervened.
                But the words
made solely of air
        or less,
                that came to me
out of the air
        and insisted
                on being written down,
I regret most—
        that there has come an end
                to them.
For in spite of it all,
        all that I have brought on myself,
                grew that single image
that I adore
        equally with you
                and so
it brought us together.

BOOK III

What power has love but forgiveness?
        In other words
                by its intervention
what has been done
        can be undone.
                What good is it otherwise?
Because of this
        I have invoked the flower
                in that

frail as it is
            after winter's harshness
                        it comes again
to delect us.
            Asphodel, the ancients believed,
                        in hell's despite
was such a flower.
            With daisies pied
                        and violets blue,
we say, the spring of the year
            comes in!
                        So may it be
with the spring of love's year
            also
                        if we can but find
the secret word
            to transform it.
                        It is ridiculous
what airs we put on
            to seem profound
                        while our hearts
gasp dying
            for want of love.
                        Having your love
I was rich.
            Thinking to have lost it
                        I am tortured
and cannot rest.
            I do not come to you
                        abjectly
with confessions of my faults,
            I have confessed,
                        all of them.
In the name of love
            I come proudly
                        as to an equal

to be forgiven.
                    Let me, for I know
                              you take it hard,
with good reason,
                    give the steps
                              if it may be
by which you shall mount,
                    again to think well
                              of me.
The statue
                    of Colleoni's horse
                              with the thickset little man
on top
                    in armor
                              presenting a naked sword
comes persistently
                    to my mind.
                              And with him
the horse rampant
                    roused by the mare in
                              the Venus and Adonis.
These are pictures
                    of crude force.
                              Once at night
waiting at a station
                    with a friend
                              a fast freight
thundered through
                    kicking up the dust.
                              My friend,
a distinguished artist,
                    turned with me
                              to protect his eyes:
That's what we'd all like to be, Bill,
                    he said. I smiled
                              knowing how deeply

171

he meant it. I saw another man
        yesterday
                in the subway.
I was on my way uptown
      to a meeting.
                He kept looking at me
and I at him:
      He had a worn knobbed stick
           between his knees
suitable
      to keep off dogs,
           a man of perhaps forty.
He wore a beard
      parted in the middle,
           a black beard,
and a hat,
      a brown felt hat
           lighter than
his skin. His eyes,
      which were intelligent,
           were wide open
but evasive, mild.
      I was frankly curious
           and looked at him
closely. He was slight of build
      but robust enough
           had on
a double-breasted black coat
      and a vest
           which showed at the neck
the edge of a heavy and very dirty
      undershirt.
           His trousers
were striped
      and a lively
           reddish brown. His shoes

which were good
      if somewhat worn
           had been recently polished.
His brown socks
      were about his ankles.
           In his breast pocket
he carried
      a gold fountain pen
           and a mechanical
pencil. For some reason
      which I could not fathom
           I was unable
to keep my eyes off him.
      A worn leather zipper case
           bulging with its contents
lay between his ankles
      on the floor.
           Then I remembered:
When my father was a young man—
      it came to me
           from an old photograph—
he wore such a beard.
      This man
           reminds me of my father.
I am looking
      into my father's
           face! Some surface
of some advertising sign
      is acting
           as a reflector. It is
my own.
      But at once
           the car grinds to a halt.
Speak to him,
      I cried. He
           will know the secret.

He was gone
            and I did nothing about it.
                        With him
went all men
            and all women too
                        were in his loins.
Fanciful or not
            it seemed to me
                        a flower
whose savor had been lost.
            It was a flower
                        some exotic orchid
that Herman Melville had admired
            in the
                        Hawaiian jungle.
Or the lilacs
            of men who left their marks,
                        by torchlight,
rituals of the hunt,
            on the walls
                        of prehistoric
caves in the Pyrenees—
            what draftsmen they were—
                        bison and deer.
Their women
            had big buttocks.
                        But what
draftsmen they were!
            By my father's beard,
                        what draftsmen.
And so, by chance,
            how should it be otherwise?
                        from what came to me
in a subway train
            I build a picture
                        of all men.

It is winter
        and there
                    waiting for you to care for them
are your plants.
            Poor things! you say
                    as you compassionately
pour at their roots
            the reviving water.
                    Lean-cheeked
I say to myself
            kindness moves her
                    shall she not be kind
also to me? At this
            courage possessed me finally
                    to go on.
Sweet, creep into my arms!
        I spoke hurriedly
                    in the spell
of some wry impulse
            when I boasted
                    that there was
any pride left in me.
            Do not believe it.
                    Unless
in a special way,
            a way I shrink to speak of
                    I am proud. After that manner
I call on you
            as I do on myself the same
                    to forgive all women
who have offended you.
            It is the artist's failing
                    to seek and to yield
such forgiveness.
            It will cure us both.
                    Let us

keep it to ourselves but trust it.
        These heads
                that stick up all around me
are, I take it,
        also proud.
                But the flowers
know at least this much,
        that it is not spring
                and will be proud only
in the proper season.
        A trance holds men.
                They are dazed
and their faces in the public print
        show it. We follow them
                as children followed
the Pied Piper
        of Hamelin—but he
                was primarily
interested only in rats.
        I say to you
                privately
that the heads of most men I see
        at meetings
                or when I come up against them
elsewhere
        are full of cupidity.
                Let us breed
from those others.
        They are the flowers of the race.
                The asphodel
poor as it is
        is among them.
                But in their pride
there come to my mind
        the daisy,
                not the shy flower

of England but the brilliance
                that mantled
                        with white
the fields
                which we knew
                        as children.
Do you remember
                their spicy-sweet
                        odor? What abundance!
There are many other flowers·
                I could recall
                        for your pleasure:
the small yellow sweet-scented violet
                that grew
                        in marshy places!
You were like those
                though I quickly
                        correct myself
for you were a woman
                and no flower
                        and had to face
the problems which confront a woman.
                But you were for all that
                        flowerlike
and I say this to you now
                and it is the thing
                        which compounded
my torment
                that I never
                        forgot it.
You have forgiven me
                making me new again.
                        So that here
in the place
                dedicated in the imagination
                        to memory

of the dead
                I bring you
                                a last flower. Don't think
that because I say this
                in a poem
                                it can be treated lightly
or that the facts will not uphold it.
                Are facts not flowers
                                and flowers facts
or poems flowers
                or all works of the imagination,
                                interchangeable?
Which proves
                that love
                                rules them all, for then
you will be my queen,
                my queen of love
                                forever more.

CODA

Inseparable from the fire
                its light
                                takes precedence over it.
Then follows
                what we have dreaded—
                                but it can never
overcome what has gone before.
                In the huge gap
                                between the flash
and the thunderstroke
                spring has come in
                                or a deep snow fallen.
Call it old age.
                In that stretch
                                we have lived to see

a colt kick up his heels.
                    Do not hasten
                            laugh and play
in an eternity
            the heat will not overtake the light.
                    That's sure.
That gelds the bomb,
            permitting
                    that the mind contain it.
This is that interval,
            that sweetest interval,
                    when love will blossom,
come early, come late
            and give itself to the lover.
Only the imagination is real!
            I have declared it
                    time without end.
If a man die
            it is because death
                    has first
possessed his imagination.
            But if he refuse death—
                    no greater evil
can befall him
            unless it be the death of love
                    meet him
in full career.
            Then indeed
                    for him
the light has gone out.
But love and the imagination
            are of a piece,
                    swift as the light
to avoid destruction.
            So we come to watch time's flight
                    as we might watch

summer lightning
        or fireflies, secure,
                by grace of the imagination,
safe in its care.
        For if
              the light itself
has escaped,
        the whole edifice opposed to it
              goes down.
Light, the imagination
        and love,
              in our age,
by natural law,
        which we worship,
                maintain
all of a piece
        their dominance.
So let us love
        confident as is the light
              in its struggle with darkness
that there is as much to say
        and more
              for the one side
and that not the darker
        which John Donne
              for instance
among many men
        presents to us.
              In the controversy
touching the younger
        and the older Tolstoi,
              Villon, St. Anthony, Kung,
Rimbaud, Buddha
        and Abraham Lincoln
              the palm goes
always to the light;

Who most shall advance the light—
                    call it what you may!
The light
          for all time shall outspeed
                    the thunder crack.
Medieval pageantry
          is human and we enjoy
                    the rumor of it
as in our world we enjoy
          the reading of Chaucer,
                    likewise
a priest's raiment
          (or that of a savage chieftain).
                    It is all
a celebration of the light.
          All the pomp and ceremony
                    of weddings,
"Sweet Thames, run softly
          till I end
                    my song,"—
are of an equal sort.
For our wedding, too,
          the light was wakened
                    and shone. The light!
the light stood before us
          waiting!
                    I thought the world
stood still.
          At the altar
                    so intent was I
before my vows,
          so moved by your presence
                    a girl so pale
and ready to faint
          that I pitied
                    and wanted to protect you.

As I think of it now,
            after a lifetime,
                        it is as if
a sweet-scented flower
            were poised
                        and for me did open.
Asphodel
            has no odor
                        save to the imagination
but it too
            celebrates the light.
                        It is late
but an odor
            as from our wedding
                        has revived for me
and begun again to penetrate
            into all crevices
                        of my world.

Ten Years of a New Rhythm

These poems were written over a period of less than ten years: the earliest, perhaps, is "To the Ghost of Marjorie Kinnan Rawlings," who died in 1953; "Heel and Toe" was written in 1961. Most of them utilize the triadic stanza and the "measured line," a discovery Dr. Williams made in *Paterson II*, beginning with "The descent beckons / as the ascent beckons," exhibited here in regular form in *Pictures from Brueghel*. I say "regular form," but, of course, Dr. Williams has adhered to no regular form since his *Poems: 1909*. With the Imagists, he practiced free verse; but in 1924 he rejected free verse ("This Florida") and sought for a controlled measure. This measure he was not to find until *Paterson*, developing the "variable foot" which produced *versos sueltos*, "loose verses," as he called them.

There was the danger that even with the "variable foot," the triadic stanza might become monotonous as free verse had become monotonous. It was "measure" that rescued Williams' verse by rhythmical variations, as the blank verse of Shakespeare and Milton was rescued by rhythmical variations of iambic pentameter. "The iamb is not the normal measure of American speech," he told me in 1953. "The foot has to be expanded or contracted in terms of actual speech. The key to modern poetry is *measure*, which must reflect the flux of modern life. You should find a variable measure for the fixed measure; for man and the poet must keep pace with this world."

Adhering quite rigorously to the triad in *Desert Music* and *Journey to Love*, Williams found that this form, even when measured, could not completely express the modern idiom. "The Gossips," one of the latest of these poems, runs to the sonnet length of fourteen lines (in form, of course, it is anything but a sonnet); "The Stone Crock" and "Poem—On Getting a Card . . . from a Poet I Love" (E. E. Cummings) use the triadic pattern with a short fourth line to fill out the measure; "The Dance" and "Portrait of a Woman at Her Bath" run in almost regular quatrain form; "Some Simple Measures in the American Idiom and the Variable Foot" vary from verse form to verse form, controlled always, however, by the measure of the "variable foot." "Tapiola" (1959), looks and sounds suspiciously like free verse.

"How shall we get said what must be said?" Williams asks in *The Desert Music*: "Only the poem. / Only the counted poem, to an exact measure:" is his answer.

As he refined his measured line, Williams' poetry continued to improve. Many critics find some of his best poems written in the last ten years. Indeed, this crowning measure of his poetic line led Kenneth Rexroth to call him "the first American classic": ". . . his poetic line is organically welded to American speech like muscle to bone, as the choruses of Euripides were welded to the speech of the Athenians in the market place."

JOHN C. THIRLWALL
The City College of New York